SEEING OXFORD
SHORT EDITION

by

Alan Crosby

A Sightseeing Guide, Map and Souvenir

Oxford Books, a series published by Walter L. Meagher for
Trans Atlantic Investments Limited
Blair House, 3 Church Lane, Somerton,
Oxfordshire OX5 4NB

Welcome to Oxford! Our guided walk will take you to all the sights in the ancient and beautiful centre of this historic city. We begin at the Oxford Information Centre in St. Aldate's. Facing the busy street, which runs gently downhill from the heart of the city, you will see opposite the late 19th-century Town Hall (**1**). Inside, is a large and richly decorated main hall, where concerts are often held. Beneath the building are the cellars of the medieval Guildhall, now skilfully converted into the Museum of Oxford (entrance in Blue Boar Street, to the right of the Town Hall; admission free).

From the Information Centre turn left, up the hill, and walk towards Carfax (**2**) at the top. This crossroads is the busiest place in Oxford, as the volume of traffic – both wheeled and on foot! – will testify, and has been the focal point of the city for more than 1,200 years. The name derives from a Latin word meaning "four ways". Here stood one of the most ancient churches in the city, St. Martin's; it was pulled down in 1896, but its medieval tower, now known as Carfax Tower (**3**), was left standing. See the brightly painted figures, half-way up the front of the tower, strike the bell when the clock chimes. Those with a head for heights can climb the tower and obtain an unusual view of the city centre, the Castle Mound and the surrounding hills.

From Carfax start to walk eastwards to the High Street. Looking to your left, along Cornmarket Street, you can just see in the distance the Saxon tower of the city church of St. Michael at the North Gate. Cornmarket Street is one of the principal shopping streets of Oxford, and has been so for centuries; the name is derived from the medieval corn market which was held here. On the right you will see a pair of very large grey wooden gates at the entrance of the Golden Cross Shopping Arcade (**4**) – which leads into the Covered Market – reconstructed from the courtyard of the 16th- and 17th-century Golden Cross Inn. Shakespearean plays were

High Street view of University Church of St Mary the Virgin, Radcliffe Camera and Queen's College to the right

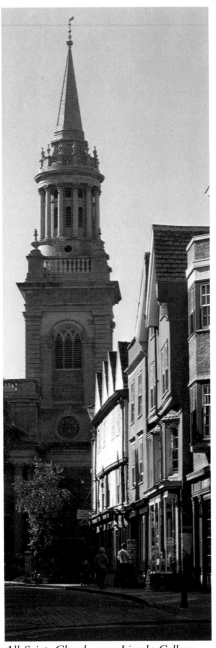

All Saints Church, now Lincoln College Library

reputed to have been held here. The arcade is extremely attractive with several small specialist shops.

Continue down High Street, which has been described as one of the finest streets in the world. It curves away from Carfax down a gentle slope, and is lined for most of its length with magnificent buildings which together make a superb streetscape. On a busy day, crowded with traffic and people, High Street's charms may be harder to see, but in the early evening or on a Sunday morning this remains one of the great sights of the world.

On the left is the delightful Victorian Covered Market (**5**), originally built in 1774. It is reached by four passageways or "avenues" between the shops of High Street. Enter the market along one of these passages, and wander round. A fascinating mixture of sights, scents and colour awaits to greet you: tempting cakes and pastries, freshly baked breads and pies, bunches of scented flowers and herbs, shiny fruits and vegetables, handmade chocolates, pastas, salamis, braces of grouse and pheasant, gleaming salmon and trout, the delicious aroma of coffee and exotic teas.

On your return to High Street continue left, past the Mitre Inn (**6**), once owned by the Bishops of Lincoln and in the 18th century the most celebrated of Oxford's many coaching inns. It was from the Mitre that the London stage-coaches set forth, a rowdy and colourful scene recorded in many contemporary engravings and descriptions. The inn retains its attractive overhanging front with bowed windows. Opposite are several 17th-century town houses, now largely converted into shops but still keeping their distinctive gabled upper storeys. Just past the Mitre, on the other corner of Turl Street, is the early 18th-century church of All Saints, now Lincoln College Library (**7**), and beyond that the lovely curve of High Street.

Turn left into Turl Street, also known as "The Turl"; this narrow road derives its name from the "twirl", a turnstile gate in the old city wall at the far (Broad Street) end of the street. There are three colleges in the Turl: Lincoln (**8**), Jesus (**9**) and Exeter (**10**). The view down the street includes the huge chestnut tree which overhangs the wall of Jesus College on the left. Opposite the entrance to Market Street turn right, into Brasenose Lane. This quiet back lane is the last street in Oxford with a central gutter, a channel running down the middle instead of gutters along the edge which are now found everywhere else. A central gutter for drainage was a characteristic feature of streets

All Souls College

throughout medieval Europe. To the left are the walls of Exeter College, to the right those of Lincoln College and Brasenose College. The large trees which overhang the lane on the left, and which in summer add so much to its shady peace, are in the beautiful Fellows' Garden of Exeter College (**11**).

Ahead of you can be seen the walls of All Souls College (**16**). At the far end of the lane you will emerge into Radcliffe Square, the heart of the University area and with unquestionably one of the finest groups of splendid buildings to be seen anywhere in the world: the Radcliffe Camera, the University Church of St. Mary the Virgin, All Souls College and Brasenose College, and the Old Bodleian Library.

The Square achieved its present form in the 18th century although most of the surrounding buildings are older than that. The centre-piece is the Radcliffe Camera (**12**), built in 1736–49 with money bequeathed to the University of Oxford by Dr. John Radcliffe, an eminent physician; it cost £60,000, a vast sum for those days. The building is circular in plan and has false columns around the outside; the large dome, at the time of its construction the largest in the country, is a most distinctive feature of Oxford's celebrated skyline. The Camera is now a reading room for the Bodleian

Stained glass window, Exeter College

Library, and so is not open to the public. The Square which it occupies was, in medieval times, an area of closely packed streets and houses: these were gradually demolished as the University and colleges undertook new building and planning schemes over the centuries. Today only the line of the two streets or lanes at either edge of Radcliffe Square serves to remind us of its ancient origin.

Turn right towards High Street again, walking along the edge of the Square past Brasenose College (**13**). Ahead is the great church of St. Mary the Virgin (**14**) the largest in the city and the official church of the University. It occupies all of the southern edge of Radcliffe Square, and its tall spire soars above the other buildings of the city as well as its immediate surroundings in a most impressive and dramatic way. Before visiting the church continue down the narrow lane, once known as School Street; notice the houses on the right and, in particular, the elaborately carved and painted wooden canopy over one of the doorways (**15**). Turn left into High Street, and here pause to look once more at the beauty of this street, with All Souls College (**16**) beyond the church, and lower down the columns and dome of the façade of The Queen's College (**38**). Between the two colleges is another of the great overhanging trees which are so prominent in the streetscapes of central Oxford and which provide such a fine setting for the golden-yellow college buildings.

As you walk past the church, notice the giant twisted "barley sugar" columns of the 17th-century south porch. Then turn left into Catte Street, now a quiet pedestrian lane but until the early 1970s a busy road choked with traffic. Pay a visit to the church: the interior, with its huge windows and splendid monuments, is very impressive. If you feel adventurous, climb the tower to the base of the spire, and enjoy the best of all panoramic views of the city and surrounding countryside from above. On leaving the church continue around the Square, walking to the right of the Radcliffe Camera. On your right is All Souls College (**16**), with its large and richly ornamented wrought iron gateways and a multitude of pinnacles and turrets. Further along is the huge west window of the college's Codrington Library. At the end of the Square, ahead to your left, go through the arched doorway into the Schools Quadrangle of the famous Bodleian Library (**17**), pausing to look back at the Radcliffe Camera.

The Bodleian Library, the main library of the University of Oxford, is one of the largest,

The University Church of St Mary the Virgin, Radcliffe Camera and All Souls College

richest and oldest in the world. In 1610 the Library secured the right to a copy of every book published in this country, and so became the first copyright library; there are now five others in the British Isles. The Bodleian has over four million books, countless papers and pamphlets, priceless manuscripts and many works of art. So large has it become that it now has several other buildings, including the Radcliffe Camera and the New Bodleian (across Broad Street), linked by a complex of underground tunnels and great subterranean storage areas.

The Schools Quadrangle, which you are entering, is so called because the different Schools of the University each had a separate section here: their names are still beautifully painted over the wooden doors around the Quadrangle. The building dates from 1610–24, and is notable for the simplicity and symmetry of its design, at once light and graceful yet imposing. Above the main entrance, to your right, is the Tower of the Five Orders, which is so named because its design incorporates each of the Five Orders, or styles of classical architecture. The statue in the Quadrangle is that of the Earl of Pembroke, Chancellor of the University, 1617–30.

Enter the glass doors behind the statue, and visit the Divinity School (**18**), across the entrance hall. The Divinity School was built in 1420–90 and is memorable for its exceptionally fine lierne vaulting, a particularly delicate form of fan vaulting, completed in 1483. The building is one of the triumphs of English medieval architecture, a wonderful setting for the exhibitions held here.

Return to the Schools Quadrangle, back through the glass doors, and leave by the entrance to your left. You will emerge on to the gravelled courtyard in front of the Clarendon Building (**19**), named after Edward Hyde, Earl of Clarendon (chief minister of Charles II, 1660–73, and father-in-law of James II). The Clarendon Building was designed by the celebrated architect Nicholas Hawksmoor, and built in 1711–15 to house the Clarendon Press, later renamed the Oxford University Press. The Press eventually outgrew its premises and in 1830 moved to an extensive site in Walton Street. The Clarendon Building is noted for its great triangular pediment and portico on the Broad Street side, and the superb wrought iron gates, a feature typical of Hawksmoor's work.

Look to your right, across Catte Street, for a good view of the Bridge of Sighs (**32**), built in 1913–14 by Hertford College to link their two buildings on either

side of New College Lane; the bridge is loosely modelled on the famous bridge of the same name in Venice. Now cross the gravelled courtyard to the Sheldonian Theatre (**20**) built in 1664–9. This is not a theatre in the modern sense of the word, but instead was, and still is, intended as the setting for the ceremonies held by the University, including the granting of degrees. It was the earliest major classical building in the city, and was also one of the first (and best) works of Christopher Wren, the architect of St. Paul's Cathedral in London, and Professor of Astronomy at Oxford. The main entrance is at what appears to be the rear of the building, facing the Divinity School. Ceremonial processions and dignitaries enter here through the enormous double doors. Inside, the seats are arranged in semicircular tiers beneath a ceiling painted by Robert Streater depicting a fanciful mythological scene of the heavens, to convey an impression of an open air Roman theatre. Concerts are regularly held here, and you may climb up to the lovely cupola for another splendid view of the spires and pinnacles of Oxford.

Descend the steps into Broad Street, noticing the Emperors' Heads (**21**). They are among the finest and certainly most familiar of Oxford's many carvings and

Earl of Pembroke, Bodleian Library

Interior of the Sheldonian Theatre

The Bridge of Sighs, Hertford College with New College beyond

statues, and were part of Wren's original design. They are not, in fact, the heads of emperors, but are free interpretations of classical figures from Rome and Greece. Their precise identity and origin remain something of a mystery. In the 1970s they were renewed after serious decay.

Turn to your left at the foot of the steps and walk along Broad Street, passing the Old Ashmolean Museum, the oldest museum building in Europe, and now serving as the Museum of the History of Science. At the corner of Turl Street look at the view to your left, with the tower and spire of All Saints filling the gap between college buildings. Then continue along Broad Street; where the separate carriageways rejoin, opposite Balliol College, look in the middle of the road for a stone cross (**22**) set in the surface. This marks the place where, in 1555, the Protestant Bishops Latimer and Ridley and, in 1556, Archbishop Cranmer – three of the leading figures of the English Reformation – were burned at the stake, under Catholic Queen Mary I. The Oxford Martyrs, as they were soon called, are commemorated by the Victorian Martyrs Memorial just north of St. Mary Magdalen Church in St. Giles.

Broad Street was formerly the site of the town ditch, called Cam Ditch, which ran along the

Cupola of the Sheldonian Theatre

Emperors' Heads, Broad Street

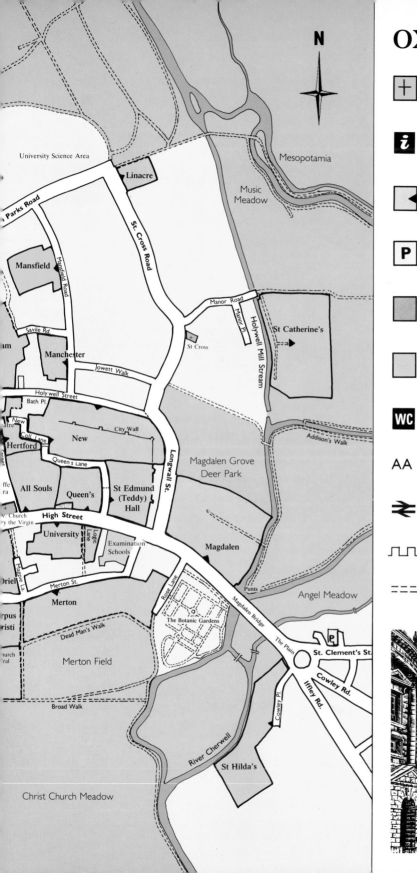

OXFORD CITY

✝	Churches
i	Information Centre
◀	Colleges and entrances
P	Parking
▪	Pedestrian areas
▫	Places of interest
WC	Toilets
AA	Automobile Association
⇌	British Rail
⊓⊔	City wall standing
===	Lanes and towpaths — places to walk

Map labels

University Science Area

Mesopotamia

Music Meadow

Linacre

Parks Road

St. Cross Road

Mansfield Road

Mansfield

Savile Rd.

Manor Road

Manor Pl.

St Catherine's

Holywell Mill Stream

Manchester

St Cross

Jowett Walk

Holywell Street

Bath Pl.

New Theatre

City Wall

New

Addison's Walk

Coll. Lane

Hertford

Queen's Lane

Magdalen Grove Deer Park

All Souls

Queen's

St Edmund (Teddy) Hall

Longwall St.

St Mary's Church the Virgin

High Street

University

Logic Lane

Examination Schools

Magdalen

Oriel

Magpie La.

Merton St.

Merton

Rose Lane

Punts

Angel Meadow

Corpus Christi

Dead Man's Walk

The Botanic Gardens

Magdalen Bridge

The Plain

St. Clement's St.

Christ Church Cathedral

Merton Field

St Hilda's

River Cherwell

Cowley Pl.

Iffley Rd.

Cowley Rd.

Broad Walk

Christ Church Meadow

Balliol College

Trinity College

outside of the city walls. Cross the road to Balliol College (**23**), with its 19th-century façade, and then walk back towards the Sheldonian Theatre end of the street. You pass the gates of Trinity College (**24**) and the attractive 17th-century cottages, typical of those which once lined many of the streets in the city centre. From this part of the street there is a good view of the Sheldonian Theatre and the imposing portico of the Clarendon Building with its great pillars. On the other side of the street can be seen Sir George Gilbert Scott's superb slender spire of Exeter College chapel rising above the rooftops.

Beyond the cottages you come to Blackwell's Bookshop (**25**), famed throughout the world. It is housed in an interesting 18th-century building, once a town house. The New Bodleian Library (**26**) is immediately adjacent to Blackwell's. It was built in 1937–40 after the older library had become hopelessly crowded and full. The "New Bod", as it is commonly known, is typical of the architecture of 1930s Oxford. Glimpse the charming elephant on the weathervane of the History Faculty building (**27**), the former Indian Institute, at the crossroads ahead.

At the traffic lights turn left and walk a short distance down Parks Road to look at the elegant façade of Wadham College (**28**), set back from the road behind a smooth green lawn. The Kings Arms, on the corner of Parks Road and Holywell Street, is an old Oxford pub which is a favourite haunt of undergraduates. Return to the traffic lights and turn left into Holywell Street, and walk along it as far as the Holywell Music Room (**29**). This plain but delightful building dates from 1742–8, and was the ancestor of modern concert halls, being the first building in Europe specifically designed and built for musical performances. Two and a half centuries later it is still fulfilling its original purpose. Holywell Street has more surviving 17th- and 18th-century houses than any other street in central Oxford, and in recent years most have been restored and repainted. A good view of the houses, with their attractive variety of sizes, architectural details and colourful paintwork can be obtained from this point, the whole street making a very pleasant picture.

Almost opposite the Music Room is the entrance to Bath Place (**30**), perhaps the most quaint and tucked away part of the city centre. It is the last survivor of the cobbled yards or courts, which were once a characteristic feature of Oxford. Its houses, which date from the 16th and 17th centuries, lean at odd angles and have pastel

Blackwell's bookshop

New College gate

St Edmund Hall

coloured paintwork. The medieval town ditch, which we have noted in Broad Street, passed through the site of Bath Place, and is still marked by a depression in the ground, which is why the courtyard slopes down from the street: the houses are actually built across the site of the ditch. Go down Bath Place and at the end turn left, through the very narrow, low arched passageway, into the garden of the Turf Tavern (**31**). The Turf is the oldest and by far the most picturesque of the many public houses and taverns in the city of Oxford. It lies at the foot of the great city wall — this is one of the best surviving stretches of the medieval defences — and close to the bell-tower of New College; the chiming of bells is well known to customers of the tavern. The narrow pathway continues through the yard of the Turf Tavern and then turns to the right, to become St. Helen's Passage. Notice here how the new buildings of Hertford College have been cleverly fitted into the cramped and confined space, a good example of the care for architecture and history which now characterizes the University and colleges. St. Helen's Passage runs between high dark walls to emerge on to New College Lane almost beneath the Bridge of Sighs (**32**). The bridge frames a fine view

St Peter-in-the-East

Shops in the High Street

Old City Wall with
New College gardens

Celebrating the end of exams

westwards to the Sheldonian Theatre, Clarendon Building and Bodleian Library.

Turn left along New College Lane, and around the double bend in the lane visit New College (**33**), one of the largest and most splendid of Oxford's thirty-five colleges. Then return to the lane and continue left under the second bridge. New College Lane is typical of the back streets of "old" Oxford and, despite yellow no-parking lines and the tarred road surface, it retains to this day something of its medieval atmosphere. Notice as you proceed by the old-fashioned lamp-standards, the towers and pinnacles of All Souls College (**16**) over the high wall to your right and on turning left, the superb series of carved heads and gargoyles high along the buildings of New College (**34**). Ahead on the right is the great library building of Queen's College (**35**), a very fine piece of early 18th-century classical architecture, crowned by a caryatid, a winged statue. Along the lane, at the next bend, the church of St. Peter-in-the-East (**36**) comes into view. This dates from the 11th and 12th centuries, and is now the library of St. Edmund Hall. The library is not open to the public but visitors may enter its impressive and cavernous crypt, one of the finest in the city.

St. Edmund ("Teddy") Hall (**37**) itself is on the left just past the entrance gates to the churchyard. Access to the library is through the delightful and intimate Front Quadrangle of the college. It is a very great contrast to the magnificence of New College, and the two neighbouring colleges perfectly illustrate the way in which Oxford combines architectural splendour with quiet beauty. On reaching High Street turn right, and visit (The) Queen's College (**38**), noting the long and sweeping curve of High Street looking up the gentle slope towards the city centre. The view from the corner of Queen's Lane and High Street includes the dome and façade of Queen's College itself, the spires of St. Mary the Virgin and All Saints, and All Souls College. On the other side of High Street is the long frontage of University College (**39**). Retrace your steps, passing the entrance to Queen's Lane, where the Coffee House on the corner is built on the site of the oldest coffee-house in Europe, dating from the 1630s. On the other side of the road is the stately and imposing Examination Schools building (**40**), built in the same Jacobean style as the Town Hall. It was constructed in 1877–83 and is used for all University examinations. In May and June the street outside is crowded with students entering or leaving

Cupola of Queen's College by night

Botanic Gardens with Magdalen Tower beyond

their examinations, accompanied by numerous friends offering good wishes, moral support or commiserations!

Continue along High Street, past the row of shops which occupies 17th-century town houses, the upper floors being student accommodation for St. Edmund Hall. Keeping to the left, cross Longwall Street. As its name implies, this street ran alongside the city wall, but the long high wall which can be seen on the right-hand side of Longwall Street is the 15th-century boundary wall of Magdalen College (**41**). The city wall ran behind the houses on the left-hand side of the road.

Ahead, along High Street, can be seen the tall and lovely tower of Magdalen College, rising high above the street, and the long pale golden front of the college. The tower is often considered to be the most beautiful in the city, and its setting enhances a fine piece of architecture. Every May Morning (May 1st) a choir sings from the tower at 6.00, a ceremony which dates back to medieval times, and which is one of the highlights of the Oxford calendar. Try to spend some time in Magdalen (pronounced Maudlin) College, with its cloisters, riverside walks and deer park (**42**). On leaving, turn left along High Street and go as far as Magdalen Bridge (**43**), the eastern approach to the city for

Deer Park, Magdalen College

Water-lilies in one of the Botanic Gardens hot-houses

two thousand years or more. The present bridge, over the River Cherwell, was built in the late 18th century. It offers a good view of the river which, in the summer, is crowded with rowing boats and that characteristic craft of Oxford's waterways, the punt.

Cross the road in front of Magdalen College to the other side of High Street, where you may visit the 17th-century Botanic Gardens (**44**). Turning towards Carfax, walk down to the Eastgate Hotel (**45**). As its name implies, the hotel was built on the site of the ancient east gate of the old walled city. Here turn left into Merton Street. Opposite the hotel entrance, you will see the beautiful wrought iron gates and splendid clock of the Examination Schools.

Merton Street is a quiet, cobbled back street, with an attractive mixture of domestic and college architecture. Until the 1970s, the old lamp-standards in this street and New College Lane were still lit by gas. On the right, around the first bend, is the rear of University College and the Examination Schools, and, on the left behind the high wall, the gardens of Merton College. Merton College (**46**) is one of the competitors for the title of "oldest in Oxford", and the charming Mob Quad of the 1350s is unquestionably the earliest surviving quadrangle in

Merton College

Books in Merton Library

Magdalen College cloisters

The Great Hall, Christ Church

the University. Just past Merton College chapel, turn left down a narrow gated pathway – Merton Grove – overhung by trees. Corpus Christi College (**47**), with its attractive pelican sundial, is on the right.

At the end of the path go through the iron gate and continue straight ahead for a few more yards. To your left is the open space called Merton Field (**48**). If you look back across the field you can see one of the best-preserved stretches of the medieval city wall, with the 17th-century buildings of part of Merton College behind. There is also a particularly attractive view of Magdalen College tower rising over the trees and rooftops. If you then look through the arched gateway on the right-hand side of the path you will see some of the private gardens of Christ Church and beyond them a very good view of the tower and spire of Oxford Cathedral (**49**), which is also the College Chapel.

Continue ahead until you reach the wide gravelled road known as the Broad Walk. This divides Merton Field from the larger and more rural Christ Church Meadow (**50**) which is ahead of you. The Meadow is a marvellous survival, a piece of grazing land only yards from the centre of a busy city. It has never been ploughed and has never had chemical pesticides and fertilizers used on it, so it is unusually rich in wildlife and has many rare plants and insects.

If you wish to go down to the Thames to see the river and its boating and rowing, there is a circular walk along tree-lined banks around Christ Church Meadow. Otherwise, turn to the right along Broad Walk, towards the large and prominent Meadow Buildings (**51**) of Christ Church, clad with Virginia creeper, built in the 1860s. Pass through the entrance gate into the college (small fee payable).

Christ Church (**52**) is the largest, richest and most magnificent in the University. Within its precincts are the Cathedral, the Chapter House and the Picture Gallery, which houses some of the extensive collection of art treasures owned by the college. The route through the buildings and quadrangles is well-signposted for visitors to enable you to see all the major features, and exits on to Oriel Square (**53**). As you pass through the college, by way of the splendid Cathedral, notice the vast Tom Quad (this is the great Front Quadrangle of the College, named after Tom Tower, the bell-tower over the entrance which houses The Great Tom bell; "Old Tom" chimes 101 times every evening as it has done for over 400 years), the statue of Mercury in the middle of the water-lily pond

Tom Tower and Mercury Pond, Christ Church

full of huge carp, and the sundial on the wall as you leave the quadrangle to the north.

To leave Christ Church, turn left into Oriel Square (**53**), passing by Oriel College (**54**) to reach King Edward Street, which is distinctly Edwardian in character.

Turn left into Bear Lane, named after the Bear public house visible in front of you at the corner of Alfred Street. Notice the recently restored Quartermaines Stables on the right (**55**). On reaching the Bear turn left into Blue Boar Street; on the left are 1960s buildings of Christ Church, neatly tucked into the limited space available. The street passes beside the Museum of Oxford to emerge on to bustling St. Aldate's.

Here turn left for a short distance to look at the magnificent façade of Christ Church, built in the 1520s and surmounted by the majestic dome of Tom Tower (**56**), another of Oxford's favourite landmarks. Then cross the street and pass by the ancient St. Aldate's Church (**57**), to return to the City Information Centre from where you started your walk.

Stained glass window, Church of St Mary the Virgin

Christ Church gardens

Christ Church Meadow

Eights Week

The spire of Nuffield College

PHOTOGRAPH CREDITS

Chris Buckley: front endpaper, and pages 4, 5, 6, 13a, 14a,b, 18a,b, 23, 24a, 26c, 28, 30b. **Peter Cormack:** page 30a. **K.P. Gingell:** front cover (a,d,f,g), and pages 19a,b, 20a,b, 21a,b,c, 24b, 26a,b, 31a, 32, back cover. **Rob Judges:** front cover (e), and page 31b. **Thomas-Photos:** front cover (b,c), and pages 2, 3, 7, 8, 11, 12, 15, 25. **Woodmansterne:** pages 13b, 27.

SOME USEFUL TELEPHONE NUMBERS:

Apollo Theatre (Box Office)	244544	National Express:	791579
British Rail (wait for reply — calls answered in strict rotation)	722333	Thames Transit (inc. Oxf. Tube to London)	772250
British Rail 'Talking Timetable' (Oxford-London)	249055	Hospital (John Radcliffe / JR II)	64711
Bus/coach information:		Information Centre	726871
Oxford South Midland — Local services	711312	Library (Central, Westgate)	815549
City Link (fast services: 190 to Marble Arch and Victoria, London; X70 to Gatwick and		Oxford Playhouse	247134
		Police Station (St. Aldate's)	249881
		Post Office (St. Aldate's)	814581
Heathrow)	711312	Tickets in Oxford (Information Centre)	727855
(Sundays and 6pm-7am	774611)		

Designed by Wendy Meagher
Photo-reproductions and studio work by Oxford Litho Plates Ltd., Oxford
Printed in Great Britain by KNP Group Ltd., Redditch